signature DIGITAL
the need of cashless society

First Edition

2017

WRITTEN BY
Akash Kamal Mishra

DISCLAMER

Digital Signature –The Need of Cashless Society is a book made for sharing the entire concepts about digital signature.

This publication is made on the condition and understanding that the content and the information it contains are merely for society awareness as a reference and must not be taken as having the authority of being binding in anyways on Publisher & Author.

Printer, Publisher & Author are not responsible for any kind of damages or loss caused to any person on accounts of error / omission in advertently crept in.

No one neither Author, Publisher, nor Printer is liable for any breach of copyright…

Happy Reading!!!!!!!!!!!!!!!

DEDICATED TO

Shri Udayraj Mishra
{My Grand Father}

&

Late Smt. Sarla Mishra
{My Grandmother}

Digital India Awards 2016

Silver

In Appreciation for Out Standing Contribution And Dedication Towards

CYBER SAFETY

Mr. Akash Kamal Mishra

AWARDED ON
28 – 01 – 2017

Neeta Verma
Director General
National Informatics Centre
Ministry of Electronics & Information Technology

Aruna Sundararajan
Secretary
Ministry of Electronics & Information Technology

india.gov.in
INITIATIVE

About Author

Akash Kamal Mishra born on 22 June at Rewa ,
 Madhya Pradesh, India which is
famous for the origin of **WHITE
TIGER** in a very small village with
a distance of 150km from birth place
named **Sabicha Post. Sihawal
District –Sidhi , Madhya Pradesh,
India.**

He has completed his entire schooling with Physics,
Chemistry, Biology from Morition Public Senior
Secondary School, Sidhi Madhya Pradesh.

He Became an author during his graduation time at
the age of 21 and published his 1st book on **An
overview on cyber crime & security , volume-I with
ISBN : 978-15-45344-62-0** now available in online
stores of amazon's .

Being an author he has been awarded by many world
famous luminaries and has been recognized as the
cyber expert in very short age. Also he has been
awarded **Young writer 2016, District Icon Award
2016** ,by the **cyber security expert of India, Inspector
General of Police Indore**, and also the prestigious
**Digital India Award - Silver Medal from Ministry of
Information Technology Government of India .**

Currently he is Pursuing B.A.LL.B.(Hons.) from Indore Institute of Law Indore, India which is Affiliated to Devi Ahilya University and Bar Council of India.

He has completed his diploma in Certified Information Security Engineer, Certified Ethical Hacker from EC-Council.

Akash Kamal Mishra started working for seminars on cyber safety and had taken 32 Seminars on Cyber Safety with in association of Indore Administrative Department, Indore and had interacted with 6000+ Students of various cities .

~~~~~

FROM THE DESK OF AUTHOR

I would like to give my sincere sense of gratitude to my parents and siblings who has supported me for this work the book Digital Signature –The Need of Cashless Society is an introductory book to understand the concept of digital signature.

In the time of digitalization it is much important to know about the working of digital signature, use of digital signature, origin of digital signature etc.,

This book deals with such topics in a simple manner so that people can understand the word Digital Signature. Let's come together for digitalization , I have faith that this book will definitely prove beneficial to all Netizens.

Akash Kamal Mishra
Pursuing B.A.LL.B(HONS.)

PREFACE

People who do business on the Internet require security and trust. In electronic commerce and communication, neither we can see the person with whom we are speaking with, nor the documents that prove one's identity. We must also ask our self: Is this indeed, the contract my business partner has sent to me or has someone unauthorized seen and changed it before it reached my desk? What will happen if I have problems with the contract, and whether I may take it to a court of law or not? Considering pace and criticality of today's transactions, there's a constant pressure to safeguard businesses against fake activities and misuse. And the availability of Digital signatures at an affordable price turns out to be imperative for a wide range of applications and verticals. In the present era, the level of risk is same for all businesses, irrespective of their sizes, which makes it essential even for a small organization for effective implementation, yet economical, measures for business and transaction protection. Online authentication became necessary in the fast growing digital environment.

Lot of different kinds of electronic signatures are available to authenticate, in which Digital signature is one of the powerful authentication method.

Digital signature not only authenticates the person, who sends the data, also ensures the integrity of the data transferred, making sure that the data has not been tampered with while it is transferred. A shift from paper-based transactions to paperless transactions (e-transactions) is no longer a painful experience. However, the challenge is to carry out these transactions in a secure and authenticate way. To counter this challenge, Digital signature technology is seen as a mechanism to maintain security and authenticity of these transactions, while making them simpler and faster.

~AUTHOR

<u>INDEX</u>

DIGITAL SIGNATURE —The Need of Cashless Society

****

I

DIGITAL SIGNATURE

Internet has brought an onset of information revolution which is the driving force in today's era. It has brought us in the "third wave society" which is bound to reshape the fundamentals of the economy which in the commencement was primarily agrarian in nature, then industrial and now in the process of becoming knowledge and information based. Many applications such as business transactions, banking, stock trading, buying and selling of goods and services over net are increasingly emphasising electronic transactions which minimize the operational costs and provide better services. These computer based applications led to phenomenal increase in electronic records. The electronic information that are generated, processed, stored and transmitted over computer networks is valuable, sensitive and is required to be protected against dabbling by malicious third party.

The advent of information technology revolutionised the whole world and fortunately India lea a leading role and captured global attention. Digital Signature provides for enabling a person to use it just like the traditional signature. The basic purpose of digital signature is not different from our conventional signature. The purpose therefore is to authenticate the document, to identify the person and to make the contents of the document binding on person putting digital signature.

A digital signature is used to authenticate digital information such as documents, e-mail messages, and macros by using computer cryptography. Digital signatures help to establish the following assurances:

(a) **Authenticity**: - The digital signature helps to assure that the signer is who they claim to be.

(b) **Integrity**: - The digital signature helps to assure that the content has not been changed or tampered with since it was digitally signed.

(c) **Non-repudiation**: - The digital signature helps to prove to all parties the origin of the signed content. "Repudiation" refers to the act of a signer's denying any association with the signed content.

The authenticity of paper documents can be made fairly by putting return signatures which validate and certify the documents.

Similarly, in case of electronic documents digital signatures serve the purpose of validation and authentication.

Validation here refers to the process of certifying the contents of the documents.[1]

Authentication here refers to the process which is used to ascertain the identity of the person for the identity of specific information and with reference to message, it involves ascertaining its source and that it has not been modified or replaced in transit.[2]

Digital signature, are nothing but a string of ones and zeroes which serves the purpose of validation and authentication of electronic documents and performs the same function as that of a hand written signature.[3]

Digital signature software became a powerful business tool in recent years that is used to sign documents, contracts, e-tax filing etc. After the UN published the UNCITRAL Model Law on Electronic Commerce in 1996 that gave uniform standards for digital signature legislation for the e-business and e-commerce most of the countries started following it. The document is legally bounded when it is

---

[1] Subramanya S.R.,"Digital Signature"
[2] American Bar Association/Digital signature guidelines.
[3] Supranote 1.

digitally signed. Digital signature law may slightly vary between countries.[4] The awareness and percentage of people using digital signature also varies between countries. In developing countries, percentage of internet users are very less when compare to the developed countries, which is directly proportional to the users of digital signature.

---

[4] History of Digital Signature Law, 2013

II

<u>MEANING</u>

Digital Signature is a binary code that authenticates and executes a document and also identifies the signatory, like what a handwritten does. It can be defined as a short unit of data that bears a mathematical relationship to the data in the documents context and provides assurance to the recipient that the data is authenticate.[5]

A *Digital Signature* or *Digital Signature Scheme* is a mathematical scheme for demonstrating the authenticity of a digital message or document. A valid digital signature gives a recipient reason to believe that the message was created by a known sender, and that it was not altered in transit. Digital signatures are based on public key encryption.

It uses prime numbers like 2, 3, 5, 7, 11 and so on which can be divided only by itself or by 1 and is incapable of division by other numbers. We have unlimited prime numbers and in Digital Signature we use the multiple of

---

[5] Write P, "Eggs in basket- Distributing the risk of electronic signature", (1995),P.30

prime numbers. Digital signature enables the recipient of the information to verify the authenticity of information origin and also verify that the information is intact.[6]

A valid digital signature gives a recipient reason to believe that the message was created by a known sender, such that the sender cannot deny having sent the message and that the message was altered or transit. In simple words the digital signature can be defined as a data which accompanies a digitally encoded message and which can be used to authenticate originator as well as message.[7]

The term Digital Signature is commonly used to refer to the situations where the text of the data message is encrypted in such a way that a recipient can be confident that it did originate from the identified sender and that it has not been subject to any modifications for amendment during the course of transmission.[8]

---

[6] www.caclubindia.com/articles/the-law-of-digital-signature

[7] Ahmed,Dr. Farooq, Pioneer books, New Era Law publications, IInd edition,2005,P.62

[8] Lloyd Ian, Legal Barriers to Electronic Contract: Formal Requirements and Digital Signatures in Lilian Edwards and Cserlotve Waelde , (ed.)Law and the Internet Regulating Cyber Space , 1997 p.147

"Digital Signature" under Section 2(1)(p) the *Information Technology Act, 2000* means Authentication of any electronic records by subscribers by means of electronic method or procedure in accordance with Section 3 of the IT Act which is as follows:

Section 3 – Authentication of Electronic records:

(1) Subject to the provision of this section, any subscriber may authenticate an electronic record by affecting with digital signature.

(2) The authentication of the electronic records shall be affected by the use of asymmetric crypto system and hash functions which envelops and transforms the initial electronic record into another electronic record.

Explanation:- For the purpose of this sub-section *"Hash Function"* means an algorithm happening for translation of one sequence of bits into another, generally smallest set known as *"Hash Result"* such that an electronic record yields the same hash result every time the algorithm is executed with the same electronic record as its input making computationally infeasible:

(a) To derive or reconstruct the original electronic records from the hash result produced by the algorithm.

(b) Those two electronic records can produce the same hash result using the algorithm.

(3) Any person by these public key of the subscriber can verify the electronic records.

(4) The *Private Key* and the *Public key* are unique to the subscriber and constitute a functioning key pair.

III
HISTORICAL BACKGROUND

Whitfield Diffie and also *Martyn Hellman* throughout 1976, were the first that explained the idea of an Electronic digital signature. They simply conjectured in these kinds of techniques.[9]

Here are some of the milestones in the history of digital signature technology:

- **1976:** Whitfield Diffie and Martin Hellman first described the idea of a digital signature scheme, but they only theorized that such schemes existed.
- **1977:** Ronald Rivest, Adi Shamir and Len Adleman invented *The RSA algorithm*, which could be used to produce a kind of primitive digital signature.
- **1988:** *Lotus Notes 1.0*, which used the RSA algorithm, became the first widely marketed software package to offer digital signatures.
- **1999:** The ability to embed digital signatures into documents is added to PDF format.

---

[9] http://www.ukessays.com/essays/communication/history-of-digital-signature-communications-essay.php

- **2000:** The *e-Sign Act* makes digital signatures legally binding.
- **2002:** *SIGNiX* is founded and becomes the most broadly used cloud-based digital signature software.
- **2008:** The PDF file format becomes an open standard to the International Organization for Standardization (ISO) as ISO 32000. Includes digital signatures as integral part of format.

Today, digital signatures are well established as the most trusted way to get documents signed online. Unlike the original digital signature technology, today's digital signatures are easy to use and can be created using any computer with an Internet connection.

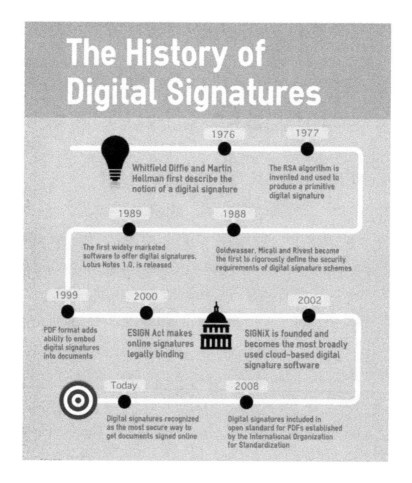

Soon after this, in 1978 Ronald Rivesc, Adi Shamir, Len Adeleman discovered the first public key encryption and signatures key now referred to as RSA (after the names of its inventors). The first widely marketed software package to offer digital signature was *Lotus Notes 1.0*, release in 1989 and is usually employed by the RSA algorithm.

IV

TECHNICAL CONCEPT OF DIGITAL SIGNATURE

(a) *RSA DIGITAL SIGNATURE*

In RSA Digital Signature, originator of a message, generates an encrypted version of the message, this encrypted version is when sent with a copy of plain text message. The recipient with the help of public key of the originator will decrypt the message and will then compare it with the plain text version. If the two are the same, the recipient can be assured that the originating system possessed the encryption key, and that message content was not changed enroot.[10] The inherent weaknesses of the RSA scheme is that encryption and decryption is to be applied to the entire message content and thus the volume of data sent becomes double.

The original message size which ultimately leads too increase in costs in terms of processing and communications overhead.

---

[10] Thomas J.Smedinghoff (ed.)online law, the spa's legal guide to doing business on the internet (1997) at Page no.103

To improve the RSA scheme, a hash function is introduced into the processing.

(b) *HASH FUNCTION*

RSA public key encryption is useful but it is slow and because of this limitation, RSA is rarely used alone. In order to save time it is often combined with other cryptographic algorithm such as Hash Function. It is seen that encrypting a document with a public key system requires a lot of time, to speed up the procedure; it is possible to apply the private key, not the whole message but only on message digest .(or Hash Code) (Asian book)

Hash Function is a mathematical process based on a algorithm which creates a digital representation or composed form of the message often referred to as a *"Message Digest"* or *"Fingerprint"* of the message in the form of a *"Hash*

Value" or *"Hash Result"* of a standard length which is usually much smaller than the message but nevertheless substantially unique to it. (Footnote)

The Hash Functions software produces a fixed length of alphabet, number and symbols for any document.

However, the contents of this fixed length are never the same for two different documents. If even one letter in the documents is altered and entirely different hash result will be generated. Hash function is also referred to as one – way function as it is a function of a data i.e. easy to compute but difficult to reverse.

It is practically impossible to reconstruct the original message from the hash result. That is why, it is known as *One – Way Hash Function*. (Footnote) From the above discussions it is cleared that to be a secure hash function the following three characteristics are requires to be present in hash function:

(a) The same Hash result must be produced every time using the same message as input.

(b) Two different messages used as inputs cannot produce the same hash results.

(c) It is practically impossible to reconstruct the message by decoding the hash result.

It is the combination of RSA and Hash Function which the IT Act, 2000 considered as Digital Signature.

V

WORKING OF DIGITAL SIGNATURE

The method through a digital signature is created and the way it performs same functionality as a handwritten signature though complex is an interesting part. The technical concepts involved in creating a digital signature are totally different from the legal realm by which they are governed. Although the sole objective of affixing a digital signature to an electronic document is purely legal in nature. The digital signature infrastructure depends entirely on the process of encryption and decryption for maintaining security. The process of encryption and decryption combinely termed as *Cryptography*.

Cryptography is a mathematical application which is used to encode as well as decode a message. A plain message also called as *Plain Text*, is encoded and converted into coded message called *"Cipher Text"*. The Cipher Text is decoded and converted back to plain text.

Plaintext   Hash Function   Ciphertext

Encryption where encoding is called encryption. It is a process which would code a message and the coded message would then be transmitted over the net. The purpose of encryption is too ensuring confidentiality by keeping information hidden from anyone for whom it is not intended.

Decryption, decoding is called as decryption. The process of reverting the encrypted of cipher text to its original plain text is called decryption. The process of encryption and decryption is possible either by symmetric cryptosystem or by asymmetric cryptosystem.

Cryptography can be classified in several ways. On the base of number of keys used to encrypt and decrypt, cryptography can be classified into the following:

(A) Symmetric cryptography or Secret Key Cryptography (SKC)

(B) Asymmetric cryptography or Public Key Cryptography (PKC)

(C) Hash Functions

In *Symmetric Cryptosystem*, it uses single key which may be shared by the sender, and the receiver of the information as the same key is used to encrypt as well as decrypt the message.

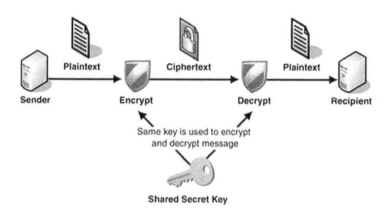

In *Asymmetric Cryptosystem*, is one in which two different but mathematically related keys are used. One key is called Private Key which is used for creating a digital signature or transforming data into seemingly unintelligible and the other key is called as Public Key used for verifying the digital signature or returning the message to its original form.

Public key is mostly used to encrypt the data and the public key can be distributed openly to anyone to encryption who needs to communicate with the recipient. And the private key is used to decrypt the encrypted data in the receiving end.

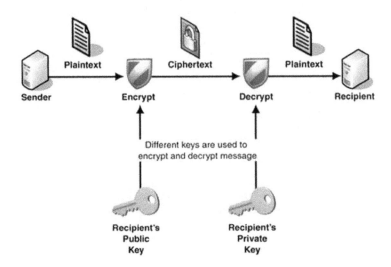

Every person who wants to transmit his/her message over the internet by using asymmetric cryptosystem must have two key. Key pairs used in asymmetric cryptosystem have been defined under the IT Act, 2000 as follows:

"Key Pair" means a private key and its mathematically related public key, which has so related that the public key can verify a digital signature created by the private key. *(Section 2(x) of IT Act,2000)*

"Private Key" – It means the key of the key pair used to create a digital signature. *(Section 2(zc) of IT Act, 2000)*

"Public Key" – It means the key of the key pair used to verify a digital signature and which is lifted in the digital signature certificate. *(Section 2(zd) of IT Act, 2000)*

The private Key has to be kept secret and if one loses its control, which in technical language called Compromise. It makes information vulnerable interlopers. The public key has to be made available to public. It is computationally infeasible to reduce the private key from the public key.

The mathematical relationship between the public and private key is such that the following holds true:

(1) Data encrypted with one encryption key can only be decrypted with other key of the pair which means that data encrypted the private key will be decrypted by the public key.

(2) It will be practically impossible for anyone in possession of one key of a key pair to determine the other key. (Dr. Farroq Ahmed,Pioneer books, published by New Era Law publications,2nd edition,2005,P.66)

Every subscriber of a digital signature must exercise reasonable care to retain control of private key responding to the public key.

A safe method for ensuring the security and confidentiality of the private key is to store the private key in a Floppy or Compact Disc or Card. It is not considered to be safe practice to store a private key in the hard disk of the computer because of the risk of it being hacked. There are methods by which the private key who are being used from a floppy or CD, doesn't enter the memory or the processor of the computer.[11]

---

[11] Digital Signature under IT Act, Dr. Gupta and Agrawal, Infromation Technology Law and Practice, IInd edition, 2012

VI

CREATION AND VERIFICATION OF DIGITAL SIGNATURE

In order to understand the process of creation and verification of digital signature Rule 4 and Rule 5 of the IT (Certifying Authority Rules, 2000) are relevant.

Rule 4:- Creation of digital Signature:

To sign an electronic record or any other item of information, the signer shall first apply the Hash function in the signer software: The Hash function shall conclude a hash result of standard length which is unique to the electronic record, the signer software transforming the hash result into a digital signature using signer's private key: The resulting digital signature shall be unique to both electronic records and the private key used to created: And digital signature shall be attached to its electronic records and stored or transmitted with its electronic records.

Verification of digital signature is a process of checking the digital signature by reference to the original message and a public key, and thereby determining whether the digital signature was created for the same message using the private key that corresponds to the reference public key.

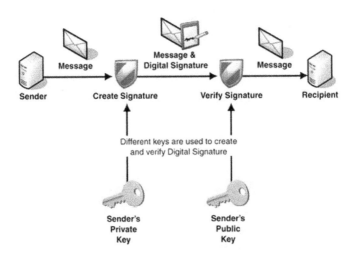

Rule 5:- Verification of Digital Signature:

The verification of a digital signature shall be accomplished by computing a new hash result of the original electronic record by means of the hash functions used to create a digital signature and by using the public key and the new hash result, the verifier shall check:-

(I)   If the digital signature was created using the corresponding private key and,

(II)   If the newly computed hash result matches the original result which was transformed into digital signature during the signing process.

The verification software will confirm the digital signature as verified if:-

(a) The signer's private key was used to digitally sign the electronic records, which is known to be the case if the signer's public key was used to verify the signature because the signer public key will verify only a digital signature created with the signer's private key and,

(b) The electronic record was unaltered, which is known to be the case if the hash result computed the verifier is identical to the hash result extracted from the digital signature during the verification process.

VII

DIGITAL SIGNATURE IN THE PRESENT ERA

- ***China's Alibaba shows off pay-with-your-face technology at German IT fair:***

Hanover (Germany): China's Internet tycoon ***Jack Ma,*** founder of giant online merchant Alibaba, gave a glimpse of the future when he demonstrated a new e-payment system using facial recognition at the ***CeBIT IT fair*** in Germany. Criss-crossing the stage in the style of a Silicon Valley pioneer late Sunday, Ma showed off the technology that uses facial recognition from a smart phone camera ***selfie as a digital signature***, saying he had just used it to send a gift to the mayor of the event's host city of Hanover.

- ***TCS issues digital signature certificates:***

Hyderabad: Tata Consultancy Services (TCS) has become the first Certifying Authority in India to issue more than ***2,00,000 digital signature certificates***. TCS Advanced Technology Centre at Hyderabad had conceptualised and led the R&D initiative to develop Public Key Infrastructure (PKI) products like digital signatures since 2000.

TCS now offers an entire gamut of PKI related products, solutions and services ranging from Digital Signature services, PKI consulting, CA hosting to PKI enabling of applications.

- ***Akhilesh Yadav launched scheme to make offices paperless:***

Lucknow: Uttar Pradesh Former Chief Minister Akhilesh Yadav launched a scheme to make secretariat offices "paperless" by obtaining his digital signature.

"It is an important step aimed at not only increasing efficiency and bring transparency in working of departments, but also to turn the concept of green governance into reality," an official release issued here said. With taking a decision to make IT and Electronics department paperless in the first phase, the former Chief Minister obtained his digital signature and approved a departmental file using the same, it said.

Using the e-office application developed by NIC, he directed all divisional commissioners and district magistrates that hurdle should not be faced by the people and students in obtaining various government services like certificates.

The former Chief Minister said the government was committed for providing services and information to the people near their doorsteps through electronic delivery system, and after making functioning of the Secretariat paperless, the disposal of files would be quick and it could be tracked immediately

- ***E-filing of I-T returns: Taxpayers to get digital signatures:***

New Delhi: In order to weed out the hassle of sending by post a hard copy of e-filed return, the Income Tax department has decided to bring in the facility of electronic signatures for taxpayers to endorse their bonafide. The Central Board of Direct Taxes (CBDT), the apex office to formulate policies for the Income Tax department, has decided to implement the new mechanism by the end of the next financial year in March, 2015.

Official sources privy to the development told that the CBDT will get in touch with the Union Ministries of Law and Communications and Information Technology to establish the legal position and technology requirements respectively before it operationalises the new protocols for the e-returns called 'ITRV'.

VIII
<u>CONCLUSION</u>

The online trading is growing widely day by day, which makes safety the biggest concern while carrying out trading by electronic means. As many other operations can be done with digital environment and internet, operation that provides identity validation should also be added to the digital environment. A digital certificate is an electronic "passport" that allows a person, computer or organization to exchange information securely over the Internet using the public key infrastructure (PKI).

A digital certificate may also be referred to as a public key certificate. When data are transferred, the user should make sure that there are no changes in the original data while transferring them from sender to receiver. And it has also become necessary to authenticate the users often to ensure security and to avoid fraud. There are lot of different ways of online identification, in which digital signature is considered to be one of the powerful way of authentication.

So, the online user use digital signature to authenticate the sender and to maintain the integrity of the document sent. Thus, it is not the scanned form of paper signature as some might think. It is an electronically generated stamp of authentication. It is a set of encrypted data used with the same validity of a paper signature, but on emails, electronic documents and online transactions. The digital signature is unique to every person as its blood group. A receiver can verify if the message came only by us and that it had not been tampered with. For now, it is quite a helpful tool but before long, it may become absolutely essential. With a digital signature, a person can file tax returns online, make investments, do your banking transactions and even send quotations to your business partners.

India is moving into a system where an increasing number of electronic transactions will go under the mandatory e-filing system requiring a digital signature. Many traditional and newer businesses and applications have recently been carrying out enormous amounts of electronic transactions, which have led to a critical need for protecting the information from being maliciously altered, for ensuring the authenticity, and for supporting non repudiation.

Just as signatures facilitate validation and verification of the authenticity of paper documents, digital signatures serve the purpose of validation and authentication of electronic documents. The private sector, too, is embracing this and the day is not far when a person may be required to digitally sign his/her job application. This technology is rather new and emerging and is expected to experience growth and widespread use in the coming years.

****